FOOTPRINTS *of* LOVE *through* OUR TRIALS *of* LIFE

REAL-LIFE STORIES OF EVERYDAY CHALLENGES

H. JOCELYN IRVING *and* OBIE PINCKNEY

NEWMAN SPRINGS PUBLISHING
320 Broad Street
Red Bank, NJ 07701

First originally published by Newman Springs Publishing 2023

All scriptures were taken from the New
International Version of the Holy Bible.

Cover artwork by glix.com

ISBN 978-1-68498-851-8 (Paperback)
ISBN 978-1-68498-852-5 (Digital)

Printed in the United States of America

We dedicate this book to our children, grandchildren, great-grandchild, and their peers with the hope that they will be guided by the Holy Spirit toward a clear understanding of a much needed relationship with God.

Contents

Acknowledgments

Writing this book did not come about without the love, support, and prayers from our families. Time spent on writing was time taken away from them, and through it all, they were always supportive and understanding of the assigned task given to us by God.

We thank God for the assignment and for entrusting us to complete such a task that proved to be rewarding and gratifying as we listened to His voice and wrote about the challenges of life through real-life stories. We as well thank Him for introducing us to Joy Scott Ressler, a true servant of God who gave up hours of her time to edit and format this book; words cannot express the gratitude and love felt for her as she offered her gifts and talents so freely.

As the book is now completed and you are reading these acknowledgments, we thank you, the reader, who thought that it was interesting enough to want to purchase it and read the stories.

May God bless us all as we face our trials of life, knowing that we are not alone and that the stories in this book are real and can be experienced by many.

Be blessed, people of God.

Introduction

History is replete with examples of individuals walking, knowingly or unknowingly, in the footprints of Jesus. In this book, you will read real-life stories that will show you that Jesus is active in the daily lives of *all* people.

So that you can go directly to stories that may be of immediate interest, the thirty-three stories in the book are organized in seven sections. It is our hope that organizing the stories in this way will be helpful if you wish to later use the book as a reference. The circumstances under which God intervenes to bring spiritual guidance or relief to His people are as varied as the multiplicity of lifestyles, and you'll notice the variations in a given section.

The first story in the first section—*Family Matters*—is about a family dealing with the needs of their young son that has cerebral palsy and referred to a Christian parents' support group, where they learned valuable lessons on how to cope.

The section *Parents and Children* includes four interesting stories that demonstrate God's love for families. In the story, *A Mother's Love*, a desperate mother in an oppressive, undeveloped country entrusts the transportation of her two young children to a stranger so that they might find a safe and hopeful life in America.

Among the stories presented in the section *Spousal and Other Relationships* is one—*A Modern-Day Miracle*—that shows how God intervened miraculously to rescue a small business from bankruptcy.

The section *Encounters with Friends and Neighbors* comprises three stories. The story, *Jesus is the Way*, tells of a laid-back member of a church who attended worship services on Sundays and, despite not participating in church activities, found meaning in his Christian calling.

The *Health Concerns* section is one in which you may likely have a strong interest. *Grateful and Blessed*, one of four stories in this section, is about two young women who, while recovering from serious accidents, developed a strong friendship that strengthened their faith and allowed God to help them heal from their injuries.

We spend so much of our waking hours on the job that we inevitably encounter stress and problems that require us to find solutions. In the *Employment and Work Trials* section, we introduce you in one of the five stories—*Seeing Beyond Our Grief*—to Ricky, who, through the intervention of the Holy Spirit, learned how to turn a pending disaster into a huge accomplishment.

The final six revealing stories in the section *Everyday Challenges* are those that show God at work on our behalf as He lives and moves among us. In *Tired of Being Tired*, you'll read about Charlotte, weary and frustrated by the restrictions on her life imposed by the COVID-19 pandemic and the relief that God provided to help her cope.

Throughout the evolution of this book, we prayed to God to allow the Holy Spirit to guide us as we sought to deliver God's unvarnished messages to the readers. We prayed that request over and over until we could clearly discern the answer to the question, "On what should this book be focused?" The resultant purpose of this book is to present a diversity of life experiences of everyday people that illustrate how God intervened to guide them to practical solutions to seemingly hopeless problems. A second purpose is to enable the reader to recognize the opportunities that God's grace offers us for spiritual reconciliation with God and the accompanying blessings.

We pray that you will be blessed by reading this book.

FAMILY MATTERS

Is Therapy for Me?

"I want my cookies," screamed Richard. The problem was that Richard was not in his wheelchair and could not get to the cookies. Mom yelled out that he had to wait until she changed Arthur, who was his younger brother. Richard resented his brother. He always felt that he was to be served or waited on first and voiced his opinion loud and clear. He was spoiled and selfish.

Richard was born with cerebral palsy. For ten years, he was the only child, and then Arthur was born. The adjustment with another child was hard on Richard and his parents. They were overwhelmed, tired, and frustrated. Richard, who could not walk, attended school daily, and a bus picked him up very early. He also received physical and speech therapy twice weekly after school.

Arthur, on the other hand, attended day care, and Mom and Dad had to juggle their schedules. The stress was taking a toll on their marriage.

They had several sessions with their pastor, and it was not going well. Each was blaming the other. Their pastor recommended that they attend a couple's therapy group that provided care for the children of parents that attended the sessions.

The next Saturday, they loaded the children into the car and drove to the class. They were met by childcare providers at the door who whisked the children off to their play area. There were ten couples in attendance. At first, the parents were not saying much but soon discovered that they were not the only ones with a child who was disabled. The other couples told them of their struggles and how the Christian-based program that they were in helped save their marriages. They left the meeting that night feeling uplifted. They were given information as to other programs for disabled children and felt like a weight had been lifted from their souls.

One couple that they met were members of the church that they infrequently attended. They told them that they would help them with the children whenever they attended church. The parents were so excited that they planned to attend church the next Sunday, and they did.

During the service, there was an altar call, and the couple came forward with their children. The deacons prayed over them. The parents went home, understanding that they now must pray together as a family. From that day on, the marriage grew stronger. Richard's behavior changed, and Arthur was no longer resented.

Scripture tells us in Romans 8:28, "And we know that in all things God works for the good of those who love him, who have been called according to his purpose." Through the grace of God, support group, and determination of the parents to save their marriage, things worked out well. Thanks be to God! *Amen.*

Chemo, Faith, and Death

Henry was a great father. He loved his wife and three daughters; they were the joys of his life. Henry was a hard worker and had worked for thirty years at the same law firm. He was well-loved and respected by everyone. He was a member of his church and was on the board of trustees. His youngest daughter was preparing to get married. The families had picked out the venue, and the service was to be held at the family church, and all was in place.

Five months before the wedding, Henry woke up one morning with blood in his stools. He went to his doctor's office, and he ordered a colonoscopy. The results were not good; Henry had colon-rectal cancer. He was scheduled for chemotherapy and went through the treatments. He, however, was not feeling any better and was getting weaker and weaker.

Two months before the wedding, hospice came, and he was rapidly failing. He called his pastor, who was officiating the wedding ceremony. They prayed together, and Henry, knowing he was terminally ill, asked his pastor to please come back and pray with him and his family.

The family gathered and met. Henry told his daughters how much he loved them and that he was very proud of their accomplishments. He told his wife how he enjoyed their fifty years of marriage and would not want his life to have been any way different.

Henry's health continued to fail. On the day of the wedding, his daughter pushed him down the aisle in his wheelchair. The ceremony was beautiful. Before the service was over, Henry asked if he could say a few words. He struggled to stand and was supported by his wife. He did not speak but prayed for the bride and groom, their families, and guests. He thanked God for sparing him to attend the wedding and that he knew that he would see God shortly. He quoted John 14:1–6, "Do not let your hearts be troubled. You believe in God believe also in me. My Father's house has many rooms; if that were not so, would I have told you that I am going there to prepare a place for you? And if I go and prepare a place for you, I will come back and take you to be with me that you also may be where I am. You know the way to the place where I am."

There was not a dry eye in the church. Henry went home after the wedding, back to his bed, and died two weeks later. Henry's story is one of faith and trust in God. He knew that he was going to die, but it did not stop him from attending the wedding. Henry was prepared to meet God. Let us also know that the place prepared for Henry is prepared for us also. *Amen.*

When I Was Hungry

For I was hungry and you gave me something to eat, I was thirsty and you gave me something to drink, I was a stranger and you invited me in, I needed clothes and you clothed me, I was sick and you looked after me, I was in prison and you came to visit me.

—Matthew 25:35–36

It was nearing lunchtime, and Ms. Smith, the fourth-grade teacher, asked the class, "Who's hungry?" The students raised their voices with a "me," waving their hands, except, that is, Gretel. Gretel was a frail little girl in the class who rarely smiled. It was noted by the teacher that she did not eat much and that she was always coughing and had a runny nose. Ms. Smith took her to the nurse, but she had no fever. A note was sent to the home with no response.

What Ms. Smith also noted was that whenever there was an event and food was left over, Gretel was always eager to take it home.

Ms. Smith was concerned about Gretel and prayed for her as she prayed for the children and their families in her class. The prayer for Gretel, however, was extra special, and the more she prayed, the more the Holy Spirit prompted her to make a home visit.

She inquired with her principal about the visitation procedures, and she moved forward. She planned on visiting the next week and sent a note home with Gretel of her pending visit. The procedures said that she could not visit alone, so Ms. Allen, the second-grade teacher who had Gretel's brother, Charles, in her class, agreed to accompany her.

When they arrived, they noticed that the house was unkempt. Ms. Smith and Ms. Allen were introduced to the other four children in the home. The mom looked tired, frayed, and frazzled. The home had limited furniture, and it appeared to not have much food because the three-year-old kept saying, "I hungry," and Mom kept saying, "Later."

They talked a while about Gretel's cough and progress and about the progress of Charles as well.

As they drove away, the teachers were heartsick and decided to stop at the supermarket and purchase essentials for the family. They went back to the home, and the mother was overjoyed and broke down. She said that the dad was unemployed and that she could not work because of the children. The unemployment compensation had not kicked in yet, so he was out trying to get food from the local food bank. The food they brought to the home was a blessing. Ms. Allen mentioned that her church had a food pantry and immediately called her pastor, who set up a delivery right away.

The family became a project for the teachers, and once a month, they checked in on them. Unemployment finally was activated, and life was better. At one of the meetings, the mom said that she would like to meet with a counselor because she felt overwhelmed and was depressed, but because of her husband's job loss, there was no insurance.

The teachers quickly connected her to a social worker, and Medicaid was given to the family.

Gretel's mom went to counseling, which helped her figure out how depressed she really was. She had no friends nor family in the area as the family moved to the town for the job that her husband had, only to find out the company was downsizing and he was let go.

The family had not attended church since they moved, and after one of her counseling sessions, she connected with Ms. Allen to thank the pastor for the food from the church food pantry.

Shortly thereafter, the family became members of the church and were baptized and accepted Jesus as their savior. Dad finally found a job, and Mom was able to put the young children in day care, and she, too, is working.

One Sunday morning, in gratitude for the help provided, Mom stood up and thanked the congregation and the pastor for their love and support during their struggles. Today, she now volunteers at the food pantry on her days off, offering food to others as was offered to her family to sustain them physically and spiritually.

Mom realizes how much God has blessed her and the family. Her favorite scripture is Matthew 5:1–10, which are the beatitudes. She knows that they are blessed and that God never deserted them. "Blessed are the poor in spirit, for theirs is the kingdom of heaven." *Amen.*

My Brother Loves Me

*And this commandment we have from Him, that
the one who loves God should love his brother also.*
—1 John 4:21

Darren and Paul, two brothers, were like night and day. Darren was humble, caring, nurturing, and loving. He was a great husband, dad, son, and friend. He attended church with his family and was very active there.

Paul, on the other hand, was not humble but arrogant. He wanted his way always and had left his wife and children several years ago and was not involved in their life at all.

Darren tried to talk to him. He took him to church and introduced him to his pastor, and Paul found fault with him, called him a hypocrite, and never went back.

This went on for years until Paul had a heart attack. As he lay in the hospital bed, he was grumbling and complaining about the nurses and their, as he said, "lack of professionalism" because they were not at his beck and call.

When Darren arrived at the hospital, he said to Paul, "Let's pray to God." Paul agreed and dozed off during the prayer. A few days later, during a conversation with a cousin, Darren was asked, "Why are you so attentive to Paul when all your life he has been so mean."

Darren said, "I am my brother's keeper." He further said, "My call is to lead all that I can to God."

Darren knew that Paul was hurting, felt like a failure, and that he needed love and support. Paul has chosen to walk another path and found out the hard way that his friends were not concerned about him. They did not visit, send cards, or even call during his illness. It was his brother and family, including his children, that was by his side and prayed for him.

Darren went so far as to ask his pastor to visit Paul. This time, Paul accepted the visit. When the pastor prayed, he broke down, confessed his sins, and turned his life over to God.

Paul said that Darren's life, too, was the example that he needed. For years, he resented him and his accomplishments, but it took the heart attack, surgery, rehabilitation, and love from his brother and family that showed him the way to Jesus.

Psalm 25:9 says, "He leads the humble in justice and He teaches the humble His way." When Paul humbled himself, he then opened his heart to let God in, and now with a new physical heart filled with the love of God, Paul goes out teaching and witnessing.

As a *born-again*, a disciple of Christ, Paul is ever so grateful and thanks God daily. We, too, must do the same. *Amen.*

You Can't Get Away

CJ and Dad went to a baseball game; it was a daddy-and-son Saturday afternoon. CJ had just learned to walk and was unsteady on his feet, so Daddy held him in a tight grip on his lap. CJ was not happy; he wanted to get down and was wiggling and squirming to get released, and the more he squirmed, the tighter Dad held him so that he would not get down and possibly get hurt.

Like CJ, we act the same way, and our Heavenly Father holds us in like manner. He protects us, covers us, and sends Jesus to save us from our selfish, sinful ways. Not leaving us unprotected, He sent the Holy Spirit when Jesus ascended, and we continue to wiggle and squirm to get out of the Holy Spirit's loving and secure arms.

We want to go it alone and explore unknown territory. The world is big; there is a lot to see, and we want to go to places that we know our Father forbade us to go that were against his teachings.

But we wiggle and squirm so much like CJ that we get away and run straight into trouble. CJ falls, bloodies his nose, and busts his lip. We fall, and our hearts are broken, our wallets are empty, and our friends are nowhere in sight, and like CJ, we run back to our Father who wipes the blood from our noses and lips, who rubs our wounds with ointments of prayer, applies the ice of grace, and rocks us with

His blanket of love as we settle back in the protection and comfort of His arms.

Our Heavenly Father never wants us to leave Him; He protects us and wants only good for our lives, but the "free will" given to us makes us squirm and wiggle away to do our own thing.

It is only when we are "born again" and submit our "free will" to our Father that we truly understand that we must allow Him to order our steps so that we can discover the plan and purpose that He has for our lives.

As CJ grows, he will learn that his earthly dad will protect, soothe his wounds, and do the best for him. He will prayerfully lead him through prayer, study, and devotion to His Heavenly Dad, where he will submit his life to Him. And then he will order and guide CJ's steps to work for the kingdom of God. Thank You, Lord, for Christian parents who can show their children the way. *Amen.*

PARENTS AND CHILDREN

A Mother's Love

*Then he went down to Nazareth with them
and was obedient to them. But his mother
treasured all these things in her heart.*

—Luke 2:51

As tears streamed down her face, Maria kissed Jose goodbye and handed him over to the man who was paddling the small overcrowded dinghy. Maria thought that it was better to send him to America alone than for him to live in a country where she knew that Jose might not survive, and even if he did, he would not thrive.

This was twenty years ago, and Jose did thrive in America. He was adopted by a family that loved him.

This story began with Jose landing on American soil. He was taken to a children's shelter by the authorities, where he was registered as a child with no name and was given the name Jose.

The director of the shelter wondered, "How could a mother give her baby boy away?"

Her assistant said, "In the Bible, we read the story of Moses, an Israelite. His mother, in order to save his life, put him in a basket in the Nile River and released him because the Egyptian Ruler Pharaoh ordered all Hebrew babies under the age of two killed. He was found by Pharaoh's daughter, who raised him as her own, and Moses grew to become the appointed one of God to lead the Israelites out of Egypt." She further said, "Jose could very well be a Moses to his people." Jose was listed as one to be adopted. Being two years of age,

Jose's language skills were limited, and he could only say a few words in Spanish. She hoped that a Spanish-speaking family would adopt him, and they did.

Carmen and Miguel had tried for years to have a child and had given up hope when their pastor announced that there were many immigrant children who were in need of a loving and caring family to adopt them.

Carmen's ears perked up, and she told Miguel, who was working that Sunday morning. She wrote down the number, called the next day, and set up an appointment.

They went in for an interview and were deemed well qualified to adopt a child. They were given the address of a shelter in the next town and went to see the director. The director immediately thought of Jose, who was now three. Carmen and her husband went into the playroom and watched Jose play with the other children. They fell in love with him, and the adoption process began.

Carmen and Miguel came by every week to visit Jose so that he would become familiar with them. The staff noticed that there was a little girl who had taken a liking to Jose and would watch and play with him during the day. She and Jose had come to the shelter at the same time. She was eight, and her name was Angel, and she treated Jose as his guardian angel.

Angel noticed that a particular lady and man were coming every week to see Jose and overheard the lady say that they would bring Jose home the following week. Angel was devastated; Jose was leaving, and she would not see him anymore.

On the day of his departure, Angel went over to Jose with tears streaming down her cheeks and said, "Goodbye." She asked Carmen, "Could I send Jose a card or note now and then."

Carmen said, "Yes," and gave her the address, and Jose left.

Years passed, and Angel was never adopted but did well. She attended college and majored in social work. She became a case manager, helping refugees and immigrants. Angel wrote Jose and sent cards to him, but as the years moved on, the notes and cards stopped. In the meantime, Jose did well and was now in his senior year at college.

One day, as Angel was clearing out her drawer, she came across Jose's address and wrote a note to him. To her surprise, he wrote back. She explained to him how she knew him. He shared the letter with his parents, and they remembered her as well. They exchanged phone numbers and agreed to meet.

When Angel saw Jose, all she could do was weep. She told him of their time together at the orphanage and how she loved him so much.

She asked him to ask his parents if she could come over and speak to them. They said "yes" but wondered why.

Angel knew that Jose was aware that he was adopted. His adoptive parents nor the agency had any info on him. They had tried but had no luck.

When they met, Angel pulled out a paper with words written in Spanish that said, "I will always love you." It was signed by Maria Cruz.

She showed it to Carmen, Jose, and Miguel. She told them that it was a note from her mother. But not only her mother but Jose's mother.

She told them the story of their departure from their country and the ride in the dinghy. She had promised her mother that she would not mention that they were siblings because she feared that they might be sent back. During their stay at the shelter, she took care of Jose, and no one was the wiser.

When Jose left the orphanage, Angel was devastated but was determined to find him one day. She thanked Carmen for giving her their address years ago. Carmen said that they received her notes and read them to Jose and wondered what happened to that little girl and why the letters stopped coming.

Angel said, "There is more." She looked at Jose and said, "Our birth mother is alive, and I'm working on papers to bring her to America."

Jose looked at Carmen and said to Angel, "Here is my mother."

Angel agreed but continued, "I would like for us to take a DNA test to prove my story that you are my brother."

Angel said, "I will not bother you any longer and pray that you will also pray over what I have said. You, Jose, along with your parents, can decide what you will do." With that, she left.

Three weeks later, Angel received a call from Carmen. She wanted to talk some more. Angel went back to the home, and they discussed her mom, who was soon to come. In the meantime, Carmen had spoken to her pastor, who counseled her and Miguel, and they were overjoyed to welcome Maria Cruz into their home.

Four months later, Maria arrived in America and saw her children after twenty years. Maria looked over at Jose and said, "That just as Moses had his Miriam, you had your Angel." To this day, all are doing well. Maria lives with Angel and has a job. Jose is in graduate school seeking his master's degree in social work so that he, too, can help refugees and immigrants as his sister. Thanks be to God! *Amen*.

Thank You, God, for Loving Me

*Sing praises of the Lord, you His faithful
people, Praise His holy name.*
—Psalm 30:4

Jordan came home from college on his spring break and said to his parents, "We need to talk." Jordan was a junior and doing well. His GPA was great, and he was enjoying his internship with a veterinarian whom he highly respected.

For years, Jordan had been hiding feelings that had been on his heart and mind. He felt that he was different and that he was not like his male friends. He had the same body makeup, and he enjoyed sports and a beer once in a while, but he was different.

On campus, he went to a counselor and talked about his feelings. He shared how he had no one to talk to and heard so many negative comments as a child about being different that he closeted his feelings for years.

During his counseling sessions, he told the counselor that he was gay and that he no longer was going to hide his feelings. He told her that he was a member of a church that was antigay and thought that people chose to be gay and that it was a lifestyle. To make matters worse, his parents were members of the church, and he feared their disappointment in him.

Thanks be to God, the counselor helped him work through how to approach his parents. On his spring break, he told them how he had hidden his feelings for years. He said that he would be leaving the family church and would be attending a church that accepted everyone as they were.

His parents listened, and his mom spoke first and said, "I knew that you were gay, but I wanted you to work it out because I didn't know how to approach the situation." His dad, on the other hand, said, "You are my son and will be forever. I don't understand it all, but I love you regardless." Jordan broke down in gratitude and cried because he had no idea how his parents would react.

That evening, Jordan's mom called a friend whose daughter was gay and asked for the name of the church that they attended and accepted all people of God. It so happened that the pastor had a parent's support group meeting the next day.

Jordan's mom informed her husband, and they attended. They were welcomed by many parents and left the meeting understanding more about their son. The pastor spoke positively to the group and prayed with them. He said that God loves all He created, that there were no mistakes in His creation, and that because of His love, Jesus died for us all, and there are no exceptions. The next Sunday, Jordan and his parents attended the church and decided to join.

Jordan went back to college feeling so light. His meeting with his parents went well, and it was a relief now to be who he was without hiding. Jordan joined the campus ministry and was so inspired by the chaplain that he applied to a seminary upon graduation, and today, with his partner, pastors a church that welcomes with open arms all God's children that wish to come.

Let us realize that whether we are Black, white, brown, yellow, gay, or straight, we are God's daughters and sons and that He loves us for who we are regardless. *Amen.*

I'm A Child of God and Names Will Never Hurt Me

Shelly was five years old in kindergarten. She loved to go to school and loved Ms. Allison, her teacher. Shelly played with her friends and enjoyed the life her parents had crafted out for their family.

Mom and Dad had great jobs. They lived in the ritzy part of town. Mom belonged to the tennis club and Dad the golf club. The only thing that they did not do in the ritzy community was attend church, but they attended the family church in the neighborhood where they grew up.

One day, Shelly came home from school and asked her parents, "What was a n———r?" They were taken aback and asked where she heard the word. She said that Karen, her friend at school, said that she was a "n———r" and was not to play with her anymore.

Shelly's parents were very upset and called their three children together. They explained to them the derogatory meaning of the word and that it was used by some people who were mean, hateful, jealous, and negative to hurt people of color to make them feel worthless with no self-esteem.

They said that it was used more openly years ago and had tapered down, but today, with so many politicians showing their true and hateful selves that along with their constituents, racism has now reared its ugly head.

When the parents asked Shelly who the child was that said it, it was noted that it was a child of one of her father's golfing buddies. That night, as usual, the family prayed together for Shelly's friends, family, and racism throughout the world.

When the children went to bed, the parents decided to go to the school to meet with the principal the next day. When they met with the principal, they told him what was said; he called in the school counselors and assured the parents that the issue would be addressed. He, too, was Black.

At the next PTA meeting, the principal brought up the subject of racism and how it was taught in the home. He told the story of Shelly (not saying her name) and what was said to her by her five-year-old peer. He informed the parents that if this biracial environment was not suitable that the school would gladly accept a withdrawal of their child from the roster.

The next week, when Shelly's dad went to play golf with the child's dad, he greeted him warmly. Shelly's dad did not shake his hand and told the group that since he felt that he and his family were "n———rs," he no longer would be playing golf with him. When the other players found out, they, too, would not play, and his membership in the golf club was revoked.

The father apologized and denied saying anything, but no one believed him. Shelly and her family understood that in this twenty-first century that racism is alive and well and that all who smile on your face do not always mean you any good.

People of God, we, who believe in a just God, must pray for hateful, spiteful, negative, and selfish people. We are told to love God and neighbors as ourselves. It's apparent that we don't love anyone, including ourselves.

What's so ironic is that many sitting in churches today are not professing love for God. They attend church weekly, give to the many ministries, and yet profess and promote hatred of different races.

God sees all and knows all. The day of reckoning may not come on this side, but when the day comes to meet Jesus, it will be done. People of God, let not our hearts be troubled. In the name of Jesus, *amen*.

I'm Just Plain Weary

Anika yelled out, "I'm exhausted." Anika, a mother of four, had run around all day doing things for family, church, and friends. Her mom needed some groceries. The secretary at the church needed help with the stuffing of envelopes and mailings. Her neighbor had a new baby, so she went by to bring a gift and got tied down to help the new mom set up the car seat. When she looked at her watch, it was time to pick up her children from school.

In the car, her daughter, Nicole, said, "Mommy, I need some drawing paper for an art project."

After stopping at the store and arriving home, it was homework, dinner, dishes, showers, prayers, children to bed, and preparing for the next day. It was then that she collapsed in front of the television and said, "I'm exhausted."

As she spoke, there was no one to hear her. She was alone, but she heard the voice of the Holy Spirit say, "Rest and relax in me. I will replenish your strength."

Anika looked over at her coffee table at her Bible that was closed. She had not read it in weeks; there was no time, too much to do. She picked it up and read Matthew 11:28, "Come to me, all you who are weary and burdened, and I will give you rest." As she read further, she felt refreshed. She turned off the television and fell back, relaxing in the arms of God.

We, like Anika, need a daily replenishment of the Word of God. We will become tired, exhausted, and even disgruntled, but when we daily refuel and replenish on the Word of God, our spirits are renewed.

Anika, when finished, put her Bible down, left it opened to the page, read, and peacefully went off to bed and slept very well. Thank You, Lord, for the spiritual food and drink that replenishes our souls with Your word. *Amen.*

SPOUSAL AND OTHER RELATIONSHIPS

Speak, Lord, I Hear You

Cora was on the back porch and yelled out to Tony, her husband, "When you come back out, please bring me a bottle of water." Thinking that Tony heard her, she did not repeat herself. Soon Tony came out with a bottle of soda in his hand and no water. Cora said, "I asked you to bring me a bottle of water when you came back."

Tony said, "I did not hear you."

Cora replied, "You were not listening."

How often, as children, did we hear our parents, teachers, and even our friends say to us, "You are not listening," and oftentimes, when we did not listen, we got into trouble?

As adults working, managing homes, and families, have we changed any, or are we still hearing "you are not listening"?

We read scriptures in the Bible like James 1:19, "Everyone should be quick to listen, slow to speak and slow to become angry." James 1:22 says, "Do not merely listen to the word, and so deceive yourselves. Do what it says." Revelation 3:20 says, "Here I am! I stand at the door and knock. If anyone hears my voice and opens the door, I will come in and eat with that person, and they with me."

31

As we read these scriptures, do they make us think about how we listen to the Word of God? Are we quick to listen? Do we deceive ourselves by pretending that we are listening as we hear the Word preached or read before us, and as Jesus stands at the doors of our hearts knocking, do we answer?

Just as Cora yelled out to Tony for the bottle of water, the Holy Spirit yelled out to us daily as we go on our walk with God. Can today be the day where we say thank You for continued knocking at the door of our souls? *Amen.*

Full-Service Disciple of God

*Come, follow me, Jesus said and I will
send you out to fish for people! At once
they left their nets and followed him.*
                              —Matthew 4:19–20

In New Jersey, when you pull up to a gas station, a service attendant comes up, greets you, and asks what type of gas you want to put into your car. Some will ask to check your oil, wash your windows, and even put air in the tire.

The service offered does not carry a price. It is a full-service gas station, and it's done as a courtesy to the patrons, and the attendants do their job well.

As those who follow Christ and call ourselves Christians, we need to take a couple of chapters out of the chapter, "The Full-Service Gas Station."

We begin with hospitality. How hospitable are we upon meeting people of God?

Do we speak to others about their walk with God as the attendant speaks to the patron about the type of gas they want?

Do we willingly share the story of the price that Jesus paid with His life for us as the attendant tells us the price for the gas?

Do we go to the Word of God and share the story as the attendant goes under the hood to check the oil and shares with us the stick that tells us if we need any at all?

Are we deflated and have not enough of the Word of God in us like our tires and need inflating ourselves?

We cannot be a disciple and not be willing to be a full-service disciples for all people of God. We must be willing to service the patrons of God and go as far as the Holy Spirit directs us to lead others to Jesus.

God assigns us all a job and has a purpose for us all as well. May we listen to the voice of the Holy Spirit and follow the course. Let us never think that we are too high and mighty a Christian and that the call given is beneath us. Like the disciples and apostles of the Bible, we, too, must go forth, offering humble, loving, hospitality to all. *Amen.*

Dedicated to the Call

And we know that in all things God works
for the good of those who love Him who have
been called according to His purpose.
—Romans 8:28

Elizabeth was out in the yard, playing with her dolls deep in her teaching and oblivious to anything around her.

It was time for lunch, and Mom called out "Liz, Liz, Liz!" three times, and no response. Mom came to the back door, wondering why Liz did not answer her call. She called again, this time louder, and Liz called back, "I'm busy teaching my students, I'll be there shortly."

Liz knew that her students needed to be taught, and that was her call and priority. There was a lesson they needed to hear, and she was determined to not let her lunchtime stop her from what she was called to do. The question for us is, when God has called us to do His bidding, how dedicated are we to his call?

Do we let things interfere with what God has given us to do? Do we stop to do something else and say, "Lord, I'll get back to it later?" Do we turn our ear to the call and pretend that we don't hear, or do we continue and follow through with our call?

God created us for a purpose, and along with the purpose comes a call designed by God that is intended specifically for us.

Liz knew her call. She was a teacher, and her job was to instruct her students, even if it meant that her lunch was delayed.

We, like Liz, must be serious about what God wants us to do. If we are unsure, call upon God in prayer and ask Him, "What am I called to do?" He will show us, but we must be open as well to receive His answer. God, right this minute, is calling your name; can you hear Him?

The old hymn by Ernest Blandly, "I Can Hear My Savior Calling," sums up the call.

> I can hear my Savior calling,
> I can hear my Savior calling,
> I can hear my Savior calling,
> Take thy cross and follow, follow Me.
>
> Refrain:
>
> Where He leads me I will follow,
> Where He leads me I will follow,
> Where He leads me I will follow,
> I'll go with Him, with Him all the way.
>
> I'll go with Him through the garden,
> I'll go with Him through the garden,
> I'll go with Him through the garden,
> I'll go with Him, with Him all the way. (Refrain)
>
> I'll go with Him through the judgment,
> I'll go with Him through the judgment,
> I'll go with Him through the judgment,
> I'll go with Him, with Him all the way. (Refrain)
>
> He will give me grace and glory,
> He will give me grace and glory,
> He will give me grace and glory,
> And go with me, with me all the way. (Refrain)

A Modern-Day Miracle

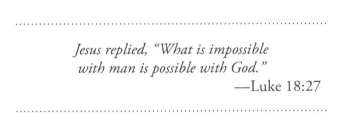

The rain drizzled and created an aggravating chatter as it splashed against the windshield of Tom's car as he drove through the early Monday morning fog to his suburban office.

Tom thought to himself that it was appropriate that he was beginning this week in the midst of a nasty rain. He fully expected that the week would bring some very distasteful experiences.

He parked his SUV in his usual spot near the back door to the three-story office building where he and his business partner, Hilton, maintained the office from which they managed their small business enterprises. Hilton was already in the office and greeted him with a welcome cup of hot coffee.

Tom handed Hilton the summary status sheet that he had prepared to illustrate the gravity of the financial problem they faced as the week began. Their automobile repair center in Maryland continued its slow but steady increase in business volume and profits, but the profits were more than offset by the operational losses by their center in Virginia. If they hoped to avoid business bankruptcy, they had to generate $60,000 in net income from the Maryland center in five days.

They were joined by Hank, their CPA, who stopped by to inform them that the Maryland Center could not generate the required funds in one week.

It had averaged a gross net weekly profit during the previous six months that was exceeded by almost twice as much in weekly losses by the center in Virginia. He made it clear that under these circumstances, they had no choice but to invest more money in the Virginia operations while they made the structural changes necessary to turn it around.

After Hank left, Tom and Hilton discussed their options. They decided to cut their losses by selling the Virginia Center even though the sales price would be adversely affected by its poor performance during the last six months. They still had the immediate problem of their accumulated debt of $60,000, which would come due in five days.

The early morning gloom and doom atmosphere were abruptly interrupted by the unmistakable cheerful voice of their business friend, Barbara, as she opened the door and burst in with her usual warm and cheerful greeting. "Good morning, boys, how are you?" As she took notice of their melancholy mood, she asked, "What's wrong? You look like somebody died." Tom and Hilton had known Barbara for about three years, and they had always marveled at her calm, confident approach to life. She owned and operated a government consulting firm that specialized in statistical analysis and polling. Her conversation was always punctuated by her vocal recognition of God's blessings in helping her achieve her goals.

Barbara poured herself a cup of coffee, and Tom relayed their plight to her. Barbara looked them in the eye and gently asked, "Have you talked this over with God?"

Hilton gasped and asked, "What?"

Barbara had her answer to her question. She calmly placed her coffee cup on the conference table and said, "Step over close to me, gentlemen," and she took their hands into hers and said, "Let us pray." For the next five minutes or more, Barbara called upon Jesus to bring His divine powers to bear on the overwhelming financial challenge that these two sons of God were facing. She acknowledged that what she was asking Jesus to do for Tom and Hilton was an impossible human feat, but she stated with absolute certainty that she knew that it was a miracle that Jesus could do. She prayed incessantly on behalf of Tom and Hilton, and she even reminded Jesus that these were two young men of good character who believed in God and were regular church attendees. Barbara suddenly stopped. She said, "Thank you, Jesus, amen." She released their hands, and when they opened their eyes, she was smiling happily. She said to them, "It is done, now get back to work."

About two hours later, Tom received a telephone call from Rick, the manager of the Maryland service center. He spoke frantically and sounded almost out of breath. "You and Hilton are going to have to get me some more help over here," he said. "This place is overrun with customers. The cars are backed up down the street as far as I can see. I've never seen anything like this in all my years in the auto repair business." Tom and Hilton rushed over to the center.

After conferring with Rick, Tom began to call his sources for additional mechanics to come in and help. Hilton, meanwhile, began to organize the incoming cars into a double-line scheme that enabled the street to be cleared. The unexplainable influx of customers not only continued throughout that Monday but grew and continued throughout the week.

Tom was able to bring in enough additional mechanics to utilize all eight service bays, and Rick managed to arrange for temporary car storage space at a used car business down the street. The customers were patient and cheerful during the entire episode. From early alarm and confusion to organization and increased productivity, the entire workforce rose to the occasion.

By the end of the week, Tom and Hilton were exhausted but overwhelmingly thankful to God. Jesus had performed a miracle. The $60,000 goal was reached, and a bankruptcy disaster had been avoided. Late into the night on that Friday, these two young partners got on their knees, prayed to God, and cried tears of joy and thanksgiving. They understood for the first time in their lives the meaning of being led by God. *Amen.*

God Will Never Leave You

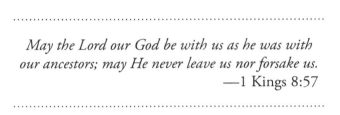

*May the Lord our God be with us as he was with
our ancestors; may He never leave us nor forsake us.*
—1 Kings 8:57

Robert was a sixteen-year-old who lived in a small rural town in the early 1950s. He secured a summer job at the boat shop, and his boss, Mr. Bill, seemed very pleased with his work. He was recommended to Mr. Bill by his wife, Mrs. Ellie, for whom Robert had done yard work at her home during the previous year. He didn't know anything about boats before he started, but he was a quick learner and quickly developed a detailed understanding of the proper techniques and mechanics of stabilizing and loading boats for towing to the buyers' destinations.

Safety was most important to Mr. Bill because he did not take kindly to having to bear the cost of damages incurred during the transport of the boats to the purchasers. Robert's meticulous attention to the details of safely loading and unloading them from the trailer impressed Mr. Bill.

About one month after Robert began his job, Mr. Bill hired another summer employee, Hugh, to work with the boat transport unit. Robert was assigned to train him. Hugh resented this for two reasons: he was a high school senior, and he was insulted by being shown what to do by a Black boy. Unbeknownst to Robert, Hugh was the son of a member of the local Ku Klux Klan organization.

Hugh worked hard at mastering the training that he received from Robert and was eventually assigned to assist Robert on boat deliveries. One afternoon, about an hour after returning from a delivery, Robert was called into Mr. Bill's office. Mr. Bill expressed displeasure in the reports he said he was getting that Robert was being abusive in his treatment of Hugh. He said he had even received reports that Robert had started bragging about supervising a white worker. Robert denied the accusations and tried without success to convince Mr. Bill that he would never engage in such behavior. Mr. Bill disregarded his denials and informed him that Hugh was being promoted to supervise transport safety, and Robert would be his assistant. Robert was crushed.

Hugh became abusive toward Robert and began to berate him for his views on school desegregation and efforts by Blacks to integrate public accommodations like lunch counters and buses. Robert was not a shrinking violet type and did not hesitate to state his views or his resentment of Hugh's behavior toward him. Their boat delivery trips became confrontational, and the older permanent workers began to give their accounts of the growing problem to Mr. Bill. Mr. Bill called Robert into his office and told him that since he refused to accept supervision from Hugh, he was going to fire him, and this would be his last day. Robert knew the futility of protesting. He accepted his pay and left dejectedly as Hugh chuckled from the boatyard.

The following week, Robert received a telephone call from Mrs. Ellie, who asked him to come over as soon as possible. She wanted to talk with him about doing some landscaping work for her at her home. Despite his bitterness at the way Mr. Bill had treated him, Robert knew that Mrs. Ellie had always treated him with respect and even fondness. He agreed to come over right after lunch. Mrs. Ellie greeted him warmly and expressed disappointment that his job at the boat shop didn't work out. She asked him what had happened. He explained the events that transpired after Hugh was hired and told her that none of the accusations that were reported to Mr. Bill were true. Mrs. Ellie told him that she believed him, but she had no role or influence in what went on at the boat shop. However, she explained that she did know that God would take care of those who were obedient to his commandments.

Mrs. Ellie walked Robert around the yards surrounding her home and showed him where and how she wanted to move some of the shrubbery and small trees. She also wanted the lawn fertilized and the walkways and porches painted. She assured him that she would show him how to do any of these tasks with which he was unfamiliar. She wanted everything completed one week prior to Labor Day. She asked him what was his hourly rate at the boat shop. He told her, and she stated that was the amount she would pay him for this work. Robert enthusiastically accepted the job.

Mrs. Ellie observed Robert's work progress closely as he meticulously followed the instructions that she had given him. She was excited and pleased about his comfort level with landscaping and green thumb type of work. The improvements in the attractiveness of her outside grounds became noticeable to all her friends and neighbors. Naturally, they wanted to know who did her work. Robert began to get telephone inquiries about his availability to do similar work for them.

One day, late in August, as he worked feverishly to complete the work by the deadline that Mrs. Ellie had given him, Robert turned and found himself face to face with Mr. Bill, who was staring at the fruit of Robert's labor. Robert was surprised and did not know what to expect. Mr. Bill smiled and patted him on the shoulder and told him he was doing a great job. Robert remembered what Mrs. Ellie had said, "God will take care of those who are obedient to His commands." He said a silent thank you to God and resumed his work. *Amen.*

God's Animals Need Care and Love Too

For every animal of the forest is mine, and the cattle on a thousand hills. I know every bird in the mountains, and the insects in the fields are mine.
—Psalm 50:10–11

The teacher asked the question to her kindergarteners, "What do you want to be when you grow up?" Many in the class raised their hands and shouted out their heart's desires to become a nurse, doctor, teacher, computer analyst, and even a pastor, and there were many other professions cited, but Michelle sat still without a thought as to what she would become when she grew up.

This question was asked many times during Michele's time in school, and now she was a junior in high school, and the guidance counselor was now asking her, along with her parents, friends, and church family, and Michelle did not have a clue.

She went to God and asked Him to reveal to her what she was to become, but she had not received a hint as of yet.

Michelle took her scholastic aptitude test and did so well that she was accepted into four colleges right away, and she was only a junior.

Michelle's parents had friends that had a farm with many animals, and for years, during the summer, they had gone there to visit, and Michelle always had a good time hanging out with the animals.

It was time to go again, but this would be the last time that Michelle would be going because next year, she would be preparing to go off to college.

When her family arrived, they were greeted by their friends but were told that there was an emergency and that a cow was about to give birth to a calf; it was a very complicated delivery, and the veterinarian was on her way.

When the family went in to get settled, Michelle wandered over to the barn and found the distressed cow who was lying down on the hay moaning. She gently began to rub the cow's back and began to pray to God to bring relief to this mother about to give birth.

When the veterinarian arrived, she, along with the families, went out to the barn and found Michelle rubbing the cow. The vet asked her not to move so that the cow would not become excited. The vet told the families to watch, and the amazing thing was that the mother cow was so relaxed by the comfort of Michelle that she stood up and delivered her calf without any complications. Everyone thanked Michele for her help. They stayed awhile with the mommy cow and calf and eventually went inside the house and cleaned up for dinner.

After the blessing of the food, Michelle had an announcement. She said, "For years, I have been asked by teachers, family, friends, and classmates, 'what do you want to become when you grow up?' I had no answer. Well, today, when I prayed to God for the mother cow and her unborn calf, God gave me my answer. He said that 'I want you to become a veterinarian because my animals need care and prayer too.' So I am going to become a veterinarian and help as many of God's animals as I can."

The following year, Michelle went off to college and, several years later, received her doctorate degree in veterinary science. Michelle gave all her accomplishments to God and said, "Through the grace of God and the cow on the farm, I grew up to be who God wanted me to be. A veterinarian who loves God's animals." Her practice before she begins to examine a patient is to pray to God for guidance. She has a plaque on her office door that says, "God loves His animals just as much as He loves me and you." *Amen.*

ENCOUNTERS WITH FRIENDS AND NEIGHBORS

An Unlikely Encounter

When a Samaritan woman came to draw water,
Jesus said to her, "Will you give me a drink?"
                                                    —John 4:7–8

Ruth had gone shopping, and as she neared her home, she moaned. She lived on the third floor, and no way was she going to make one trip with four bags. She wished now that she had left the potatoes in the store. They were on sale, and she bought them, forgetting that she had many flights to walk.

Ruth parked her car, got out, opened the trunk, and sighed. In the meantime, Art was on his way home to shower and prepare himself for a meeting.

When he arrived home, he parked his car and noticed that his neighbor was staring at her truck. He came over and asked was she all right. She explained that she had bought too much and was deciding what to bring up and what to leave in the trunk. Even though Art was in a hurry, he offered to help. He gathered two bags, and Ruth grabbed two, and they made their way up to the third floor. As they climbed the stairs, Ruth kept saying thank you and that she was so appreciative of Art's kindness. When they reached her door, she fumbled so much that she dropped her keys.

Time was fleeting for Art, but the gentleman that he was didn't say anything; he picked up the keys, Ruth opened the door, and they put the bags on the counter. She again thanked Art. As he was turning to walk away, he noticed that her Bible was open. He asked, "Do you read the Bible?"

"Of course," she said, "every day."

Art replied, "I used to read the Bible and attend church regularly, but I got tired and stopped. Do you believe what is in it?"

Ruth stopped putting her food away, picked up her Bible, and said to Art, "Listen to this." She read Psalm 23. When finished, she said, "The Lord is our shepherd, He guides and leads us daily through the Holy Spirit." She quickly turned to the book of Acts and read the second chapter about the descending of the Holy Spirit. She then turned more pages and found Matthew chapter 11, where Jesus said, "Come to me all you who labor, tired, carrying heavy loads, I'll give you rest." She then looked at Art and said, "This book is filled with messages and stories that guide us. Do you know that I did not know how I was going to get my groceries up these stairs? But I was praying as you drove up, and you stopped and helped me. God answered my prayer through you."

She said to him, "By the way, I don't know your name."

He said, "Art."

She said, "Art, you said you used to read your Bible and attended church and stopped. You asked me if I believed, and I said yes. Art, God is real, this life is real yet temporary. I say to you today, take a step forward with God, pick up your Bible, attend a church, and find a Bible study partner, and you will see life differently. As a matter of fact, my older brother is seeking someone with whom to study, here's his number, give him a call."

With that, Art left and promised to call her brother, which he did, and they have been prayer and Bible study partners now for over ten years. When Art fell away from church and God, Ruth helped him get back and, through her gentleness, led him to a brother in Christ that took him further.

There are many Arts out in the world who have walked away. Let us, through our humble approach, lead others back to God. People are hungry and need to be fed, not with a full-course meal but with an appetizer first. Let the appetizer we offer be refreshing and delectable. God's Word contains it all. Bon appétit! *Amen.*

Jesus Is the Way

Paul was a member of a large church. He attended regularly, but that
was all that he did. There was no participation in any of the church
organizations or ministries, yet Paul thought of himself as a great
Christian. He was baptized, put his offerings on the plate, gave to
special ministry events, and was an overall good Christian man in his
eyes and the eyes of his like-minded friends.

Paul was one day approached by the pastor to help an older gentleman of the church to his car. When the man tried to start his car,
it would not work. Now Paul was a mechanic and knew a lot about
cars and told the gentleman that he would take him home and have
the car towed in to the shop the next day.

As promised, Paul had the car towed. While fixing the car, he
saw a book on the seat with the title *I Am the Way*. Paul began flip-
ping through the book; it was about Jesus and His being on the way
to God and heaven. When he finished the car, he called the old gentleman and asked if he could bring his car back and will he be home
in the evening. The man was pleased and said, "Sure."

When Paul hung up, he could not get the book nor the few
stories that he read out of his mind. He knew that Jesus died on the
cross; after all, he was a member of his church since he was a child.

Yet even though he was baptized, he had not accepted Jesus as his Lord and Savior nor committed his soul to Him.

After work, he went to the old man's home to drop off the car and keys. The old man invited him in, thanked him, and asked Paul what he owed him. Paul said it was no charge. The man was very thankful and said, "I have something for you," and it was a copy of the book that Paul had glanced over in the car.

The old man said, "My son, I wrote this book over thirty years ago. I have never charged a dime for it, and I give it away because I want everyone to know that Jesus is the way." He said, "Paul, I see you at church a lot, but I don't see you in the church working for the kingdom of God. You are young and can do a lot for God in building up His Kingdom."

He opened the book and read John 14:6, "I am the way, the truth, and the life; no one comes to the Father except by way of me." He said, "Paul, do you understand what I just read?"

Paul lowered his head and said, "Yes."

He told the old man that he had tried from his baptism to walk with Jesus and had not made a commitment nor turned his life over to Christ. The old man asked could he pray for him.

He said, "Yes."

After the old man's prayer, Paul prayed and, in the midst of his praying, broke down in tears and accepted Jesus as his savior. From that day on, Paul has been walking with the Lord and has not turned back.

Paul went home and stayed up all night reading the book. He bought several copies and began to hand them out to his friends, sharing the message that Jesus is truly the way, the truth, and the life. *Amen.*

Seeing What God Sees

But the eyes of the Lord are on those who
fear him, on those whose hope is in his.
—Psalm 33:18

It was nearing time for Bernice's solo. She had practiced "Blessed Assurance" by Fanny Crosby, a well-known Christian hymn writer, all week and was ready. She went up to the microphone, prayed, and with eyes focused on the cross in the back of the church, she began to sing.

"Blessed assurance, Jesus is mine. Oh, what a foretaste of glory divine. Heir of salvation, purchase of God. Born of His Spirit, washed in His blood."

When it came to the chorus, Bernice broke down. The congregation looked at her as to what had happened? Why was she crying? Bernice was a pediatrician who loved her patients. She was on the board of trustees at the church. She was active in her condo association. Things from the outside looked good, so why was she crying?

Bernice could no longer hide the fact that she did not love Willis. Over the past few months, as the wedding neared, she was becoming more stressed. She prayed and went to a counselor, and her feelings did not change, and here, she was singing "Blessed Assurance Jesus Is Mine," and she was not being truthful to Jesus or Willis.

Many wondered that morning what had happened and had all kinds of thoughts, but Bernice said nothing and sat down.

After service, she met with her pastor, who counseled her to be truthful and tell Willis how she felt. She also had to tell her parents, bridal party, caterers, photographer, and the rest. Money had been spent in the planning, but they had contracts that had a three-month window, so with God and proper planning, it all would work out.

On her way home from church, Bernice called Willis and said they needed to talk. She asked him to meet her at the local diner. When he saw her, he said that she looked horrible. Willis thought that she was physically sick. She assured him that was not the case. She did not hesitate and jumped right in and shared her feelings. Willis said that he suspected something was wrong because over the past few months, she had changed, and she had.

Bernice knew that she wanted to marry a man who was in the church like her, and Willis was not. She had prayed to God for a Christian man, and Willis did not profess God as His Savior. Willis never attended church with her, no matter how many times she asked him. Her parents had mentioned it to her as well. Willis didn't want marriage counseling with her pastor but did so because it was required if they were getting married in her family church.

When Bernice finished, Willis said he was okay with her decision. There was no "I'm upset," just "okay." She took off her engagement ring and gave it back to Him. He took it. She also said that she would call the vendors because she knew that he had a history of procrastinating and money invested would be lost.

She went next to her parent's home and told them. They supported her decision and prayed with her. While there, she called her bridal party and arranged to meet with them the next week. The meeting went well, and they, too, prayed with her and were happy that they had not gotten their dresses yet.

When Bernice called the last vendor, she felt a flood of relief over her spirit. She thanked God for leading her in making the right decision and asked the Holy Spirit to send the man that would be approved by God.

Eight weeks later, Bernice asked the choir director if she could finish her solo; she said yes. The following Sunday, the new, happy, and relieved-from-stress Bernice stood in front of the microphone, prayed to God, and with eyes focused on the cross, sang from her soul the words.

"Blessed assurance, Jesus is mine. Oh, what a foretaste of glory divine. Heir of salvation, purchase of God. Born of His Spirit, washed in His blood. Perfect submission, all is at rest. I, in my Savior, am happy and blessed. Watching and waiting, looking above. Filled with His goodness, lost in His love. This is my story, this is my song. Praising my Savior all the day long. This is my story, this is my song, praising my Savior all the day long," *amen.*

HEALTH CONCERNS

You Are Not Alone

Even though I walk through the darkest
valley, I will fear no evil, for you are with me;
your rod and your staff, they comfort me.
                                        —Psalm 23:4

Sally was not feeling well with constant headaches. She scheduled an appointment at her doctor's office. He listened to her as she explained her feelings and symptoms. After an examination, he sent her to the neurologist for a consult and evaluation. The neurologist ordered a brain scan, it was done that day, and she was scheduled to come back in three weeks. She no sooner left the office than the neurologists called and scheduled her to come back the following day.

Sally was nervous and very concerned, so she called her sister, Ruth, and asked her to go with her to the appointment. The next day, when the nurse called her name, she went in expecting to hear some grim news. The doctor explained that he saw a dark spot on her brain and that he wanted to explore further with a biopsy. Sally agreed, and the next week, with Ruth by her side, the biopsy was done. On the way home, Sally shared her fear. Ruth asked her if she had spoken to a counselor and prayed to God with anyone. She said, "No."

Ruth asked if she would go with her to her church and meet her pastor. She agreed. Unbeknownst to Sally, her sister's pastor had also gone through the same experience. He had brain cancer, received his treatments, and has been in remission for five years.

Ruth introduced Sally to Pastor Mike, and she sat with him. He shared his story and prayed with and for her. He went so far as to refer her to a support group in the church. She left the meeting feeling much better.

The following week, she began her chemotherapy. After the treatments ended, she went into remission and has been there for six years.

Sally now works as a counselor for the cancer treatment advisory council and, by the grace of God, shares her story and walks with those who are going through it. She prays daily with her hands raised up toward heaven. Thank You, God, for the healing. *Amen.*

Leading Others to Jesus

*Even there Your hand will guide me, and
Your right hand will hold me fast.*
—Psalm 139:10

April left the oncologist's office feeling relieved. Chemo was over, and she was in remission. The doctor said, "See you in six months. April was so happy to hear the word *remission* that she floated out of the office.

From there, life was fine, and things were going well. In year one, post-chemotherapy, her labs were great, and for the next four years, all went well. At the beginning of year six, April began to experience feelings of tiredness. She went in for her checkup, and after her labs and scans, her doctor said that cancer had returned. April was upset; she had followed all the doctor's orders, yet that nasty cancer had returned.

Chemotherapy was scheduled, and April began the weekly treatments.

Up until this time of her life, April never attended church. Her parents never took her as a child, and the few services that she attended were occasional marriages or funerals.

The technicians at the chemotherapy center were very nice, and one asked if she attended church or had a pastor. April said, "No." She asked if she could pray with her, and she agreed. The prayer ended, and April felt no different than before.

The technician always greeted her nicely with each appointment, but April said no to any other prayer.

About nine weeks into her treatments, she met another patient named Michael, who was undergoing chemotherapy as well. He casually talked to April each time they met. Michael began to show a personal interest in April and began to ask questions. She became interested in Michael and answered his questions. Their time together at the center brought joy to both of their spirits, so much so that Michael invited her to his young adult group at church. She attended and had a great time.

Over time, she and Michael became good friends and began to date. They soon fell in love, but since both were now cancer survivors for the second time, they sought counsel from Michael's pastor.

He met with them several times. On Sunday, April received the Right Hand of Fellowship, accepted Jesus as her Lord and Savior, and was baptized.

Their love and relationship grew. Michael asked April to marry him, and she said yes. They had a great wedding and found out that they were expecting a child after six months.

The pregnancy went well until the eighth month, when April was not feeling well, and it was discovered that cancer had returned. She could not receive chemotherapy because of the baby. As she grew weaker, it was decided that she would need a cesarean; it was scheduled for the next day. The pastor of the church came by before the surgery and prayed with April and Michael and asked God to protect the baby, Elizabeth Grace, as well. During the cesarean, April was so weak and tired that she died.

Michael took Elizabeth Grace home, and April's family helped to raise her. When Elizabeth Grace was six years old, Michael was no longer in remission, and after a battle with cancer for a year, he died and joined April in heaven.

Before he died, he left Elizabeth Grace in the care of his sister. Elizabeth Grace was told many things about her parents and how they loved God and were happy to have conceived such a wonderful child.

Today, like her parents, she is active in her church and is thankful to God for her salvation and blessing her with a mother who sacrificed her life to bring her into the world and a father who cared for her until he died.

As we hear this story of two, who found love even at their lowest point, we see that they never faltered and trusted God to the end. Let us, too, trust God to our end as well. Thank You, Lord, for the journey. *Amen.*

Grateful and Blessed

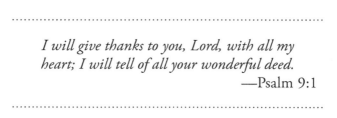

I will give thanks to you, Lord, with all my heart; I will tell of all your wonderful deed.
—Psalm 9:1

Sarah was a great student and was on the honor roll. One day, at school, Sarah was walking down the hallway when a group of boys ran into her and knocked her down. She could not get up and was hospitalized with a fractured hip and needed surgery. The boys apologized, but their apology was not well received. Sarah was upset and did not hold back on her feelings.

Her mom explained to her that it was an accident and that the boys were sorry and were punished by the principal. After her surgery, Sarah had to go to a rehabilitation center to learn to walk again with a brace as well as a walker.

Sarah's therapy was not going well because she was always complaining. One day, a young girl by the name of Erica was in therapy at the same time. She watched Sarah, and after their session, she went to Sarah's room.

She told Sarah her story about how she's had lost both legs because of a car accident and how blessed she was to be alive. She said, no matter what it took, she was going to walk again, and *can't* was not in her vocabulary.

Sarah listened and nodded her head; Erica left and yelled back, "I'll see you tomorrow in therapy."

The next day, Sarah saw Erica but said nothing, but she watched Erica as she pushed hard with her prosthetics.

When Sarah went back to her room, she cried and prayed to God a prayer of thanks for her two legs, regardless of how weak they were.

The next day, she tried hard to do her best in therapy, and each day, she grew stronger. What she noticed was that Erica was doing better as well.

They began to gather together at night to pray and read scriptures from the Bible and became great friends. They also realized that they went to the same school.

What really clinched their relationship was that they were discharged on the same day and were able to walk out of the rehabilitation center together.

Twenty years later, Sarah and Erica are still friends. Both are married and have supporting husbands and one child each. They attend the same church and help each other out when needed.

They often reminisce about their first encounter and from where God has brought them. "Grateful and blessed" are the words they use to describe their walk with God. What word or words would you use? *Amen.*

Answered Prayers

Miguel was a fun-loving little boy who never complained and was well-liked by his classmates.

Miguel was, however, not well. He had kidney failure and was on dialysis three times a week. The doctor told the parents that what Miguel needed was a kidney transplant. They prayed day and night for a donor, and everyone in the family was tested, but no one matched him.

His schedule was very tiring and tedious. He attended school in the morning and dialysis on Monday, Wednesday, and Friday after school.

He wished to attend after-school activities but could not, as he was always at dialysis. This schedule went on for years.

When he was thirteen, his parents received a call from the hospital that there was a kidney, and it was a perfect match for Miguel. His mom was excited and said out loud as she prepared herself to go to the hospital. "My prayers have been answered."

When the call came, Miguel was at school, Dad and Mom were at work, and his siblings were at the babysitter. Mom got everyone in place and made her way to the school to pick up Miguel. They met Dad at the hospital, where the team was waiting for him. They whisked Miguel off and told the parents that they would be in touch and that it would take about three hours.

Three hours passed, and the parents became nervous. They held hands and prayed to God for the surgery to go well. Finally, four hours after the surgery began, the surgeon came out and said that the surgery went well and that they could see him for a few minutes.

Miguel was groggy but awake. The parents prayed with him, kissed him goodnight, and went home. They planned to come back in the morning.

That night, the phone rang; it was the hospital. Miguel had begun to hemorrhage and needed surgery to stop the bleeding right away. They gave permission and headed back to the hospital. Thank God grandma was with them, and they left the other children with her. All the way to the hospital, they prayed to God for the healing of Miguel.

The surgery took two hours. It was touch and go throughout the night, but his parents never stopped praying.

His dad said to Mom, the scripture says in James 5:16, "The prayer of a righteous person is powerful and effective." They knew that they were faithful Christian parents. They believed in the power of prayer and what God could do, and thanks be to God, their prayers worked.

Miguel was in the hospital for two weeks; the transplant worked, and today, Miguel attends all the after-school activities that he could not attend before his kidney transplant and is doing very well.

Miguel's story tells us that God answers prayers and that the prayers of the righteous are definitely heard. Thank You, God, for the healing. *Amen.*

EMPLOYMENT AND WORK TRIALS

God—the Safety Net for the Righteous

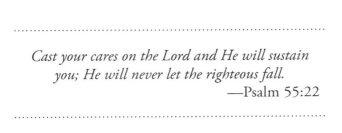

*Cast your cares on the Lord and He will sustain
you; He will never let the righteous fall.*
—Psalm 55:22

Arthur had decided a few months ago that he would read the book of Psalms in the Bible. He read a chapter each day. Today, he read Psalm 55:1–22 and stopped on verse 22, "Cast your cares on the Lord and He will sustain you; He will never let the righteous fall." Arthur closed the Bible and reflected on the previous day.

The bank manager called him to the office and said that there was a rumor that Arthur was stealing money from the bank. Arthur was upset and taken aback because he had worked at this bank for seven years and five for a previous bank. He had never received a complaint. The bank manager said that a teller told him that she saw Arthur tuck some money in his pocket when he came out of the vault.

Arthur was shaken. He told the manager that he had not done such a thing and that he was not a thief. Arthur was a trustee in his church and head counter for the Sunday offerings. If this lie got out, it would be devastating to his reputation, and he would no longer be trusted. The manager said that he would have to sit behind a desk for a few days until they looked at the camera tapes and counted the money.

Arthur had an idea who it was that lied on him. It so happened that three months ago, Amy, a coworker, had invited him to go out after work with a group. He went with them and had a nice time. He did not drink alcohol but noticed that all the office crew drank and became a little too loose for his liking.

Amy came over to him and asked him to dance. He did, and she became a bit too friendly. He begged to be excused, informing them that he had an early board meeting at church the next day, and left.

The next Monday, everyone was talking about Friday night and the good time they had. They planned to do the same the following Friday, but Arthur said that he was not available. Amy became upset with him and asked, "Why? Do you think you are better than us because you don't drink?"

Arthur said, "Of course not," and walked away. He noticed afterward that he was given the cold shoulder, and now three months later, he was being questioned about some money that he was seen putting into his pocket.

He opened the Bible and read verse 22 again, "Cast your cares on the Lord and He will sustain you; He will never let the righteous fall." He prayed, "Lord God, you know that I have not taken a penny from the bank, please rectify this matter. Thank You for Your Love." When he finished praying, he remembered that he had gone to the neighborhood store for a soda and shoved the change in his shirt pocket, and when he went back to work, remembered it and switched pockets. Maybe that's what was observed.

The next day at work, he sat behind the desk, answering the phone. He asked if the manager had counted the money yet. The manager said that he was waiting for the head teller's report. Arthur told the manager about his thoughts that someone might have possibly seen him removing the change from his shirt to his pants pocket, and the manager said he would review the tape.

Arthur was growing more distressed, and that evening, after Bible study, he asked the pastor could he speak with him. The pastor said, "Of course," and Arthur told him the story. The pastor said he believed him and prayed. When he had finished, he asked Arthur to go home and read Psalm 55:22. It says, "Cast your cares on the Lord and He will sustain you; He will never let the righteous fall." Arthur was taken aback and told the pastor that this scripture had been placed in his heart for the last two days. The pastor said, "Go home, God's got this all worked out."

The next day, the manager came to Arthur and apologized. He said that the tape showed exactly what he had said about the money that was taken from the shirt pocket and placed in his pants pocket. Also, he said that the vault money was balanced out as well.

Arthur closed his eyes, thanked God, and went back to his tellers' booth, saying repeatedly, "Thank You, Jesus!" *Amen.*

Second and Third Chances

The waiter brought the bill to the table. There were six who came to lunch. Matthew took the bill and said, "I'll pay for this, as you all know, I make more money than anyone else here." The group gladly obliged Matthew and his ego, thanked him, and left.

Matthew had a big ego. He was, as he felt, a self-made man. He and his four siblings had a very poor beginning, having been raised by a single mom. As a child, he envied his friends who had more and swore that when he grew up that he would never be poor or in want of anything.

Matthew did well in school and went to college with scholarships and financial aid. He did so well that he landed a great job upon graduation and began climbing the corporate ladder of success. He was building a nice nest egg.

With all that Matthew achieved, he was lonely, unhappy, not married, and had no girlfriend. Many of his coworkers were married, and on their desks, there were pictures of their families, and he envied them.

His place of employment held their annual picnic in June. It was always an elaborate event. Matthew had not attended over the past few years but decided this year to attend.

He was enjoying a conversation with his boss when he noticed a young woman who he had not met before. He pointed her out to the boss, who told him that the young woman was his daughter and that she was coming back to live in the town and work for the company. After all, she would inherit it when he died.

As the picnic progressed, Matthew introduced himself to Sarah, and they exchanged the usual niceties. Matthew began to notice Sarah at the office and asked her to lunch. Lunch evolved into dinner, and dinner into a relationship. Sarah was beginning to fall in love with Matthew but always noted that he spoke about himself and his accomplishments. He did not attend church, nor was it on his radar. He felt that, during his lean years, as he struggled, God did not help him. The relationship, however, did not work out, and Sarah moved on.

Matthew kept working hard day and night, seeking to make vice president. What Matthew had neglected over the years was his health. One morning, as he prepared for work, he felt chest pains and neglected them until he collapsed at the office. Matthew had a heart attack. Surgery was required, and upon discharge from the hospital, he went to a rehabilitation center to recuperate. While there, no one from the office visited. He ran out of sick days, and his nest egg had dwindled down to almost nothing; he was broke and alone.

The chaplain from the nursing home came to see him. She talked about her prayer life, and he admitted that he had never prayed and that God had not done anything for him. She explained to Matthew that he was alive because of God and the heart attack that he had sustained was so severe that most who experienced it did not survive. She came back several times and prayed with Him.

In the meantime, Sarah, who felt guilty about not sending a card or visiting, decided to go to the rehabilitation center. Matthew was so happy to see her and told her of the chaplain's visits and prayers. He said that when he was able to leave the center that he would attend church with her.

With the help of the chaplain, Sarah and the heart attack, Matthew made a change in his life. He became very thankful and grateful and accepted Jesus as his Savior.

Sarah introduced him to her cousin, Beth, and they hit it off right away. Today, Matthew is very thankful to God and shares his story. He works for another company, is happily married to Beth, and is raising his two sons. With his family, he attends church regularly. He keeps his appointments with his doctors, and his health has greatly improved.

During family prayer, he thanked God for showing him that his achievements were accomplished only through the grace, love, and favor of God. He ends his prayers with thank You, God, for second and even third chances. *Amen.*

Take the Initiative
Do Something for Yourself

*Fight the good fight of the faith. Take
hold of the eternal life to which you were
called when you made your good confession
in the presence of many witnesses.*
—1 Timothy 6:12

Justin was on a job that he truly disliked. He knew that there was something better for him that was in line with his degree. He went to the altar at his church and prayed to God and then sat, waiting and thinking about the great job that God was going to send him. Well, he waited and waited and waited each year, getting older and older and older.

During his waiting, technology changed, and zoom was introduced. He began working from home with access to the internet and could have used his time wisely to search for a job and did nothing to help himself. Companies were holding interviews online; job fairs were held with social distancing, and he did not attend. He said that he was waiting on God.

Well, nine years passed, and Justin finally realized that his skills were antiquated, and his age was a deterrent to his finding a job. He became depressed and blamed God for his not securing a job. He retired with minimal benefits, all because he did not step up to help himself.

Justin's story is the story of many. They sit back and wait for God to come through with what is asked and do nothing to help themselves. God is a giving God; He is willing to supply our needs. Justin did not help himself and ended up disappointed with the outcome of his life.

God answers prayers, but we must be proactive and seek out what the Holy Spirit sends us. The problem is that we are deaf to the voice of the Spirit. Many have not advanced in their careers because they have sat back and waited for God, who has already spoken. Scripture says, "Anyone that has an ear. Listen to what the Spirit is saying." It's time to tune into the Spirit; time is passing, and we are not getting any younger.

Thank You, Lord, for speaking loud enough so that we can hear Your plans for our lives as we grow older. *Amen.*

Seeing Beyond Our Grief

Come to me, all you who are weary and burdened,
and I will give you rest. Take my yoke upon you
and learn from me, for I am gentle and humble
in heart, and you will find rest for your souls.
For my yoke is easy and my burden is light.
—Matthew 11:28–30

Ricky was a great painter and, at every opportunity, was willing to share his artistic abilities. He was so well thought of in the town where he lived that he was commissioned to paint a mural that depicted his vision of the town. Immediately, he began to sketch pictures and took them to the town council. They approved his drawings, and he was on his way.

On the outskirts of town, he chose a site that would be a great sign of welcome to all newcomers. Ricky was set and ready to work.

One day, he sketched out all the designs. At five o'clock, he put down his brushes, packed up, left his paints at the site, and went home. The next morning, Ricky was up early, eager to resume his painting. Upon arrival, he noticed that his box of painting tools had been moved, and his designs were splattered with paint.

He was upset and in great despair. His work had been violated, and he was not happy. He went to the town council and shared the news. They, too, were distraught. Ricky left the meeting and went home feeling down. He ate dinner and just sat, staring off into space. He dozed off, and the Holy Spirit came to him in a dream and said,

"All is not lost, you have been given a gift of drawing, go back, take a look at your mural again, and turn it around."

The next morning, he slowly went to the site not knowing what to expect. The mural looked the same. He took the mural as instructed by the Holy Spirit and turned it around. What he saw was a design that he could paint over. In his enthusiasm, he ran back to the town council, shared his new vision and designs, and the end result was a better picture than before.

The next month, the council had an unveiling, and the people of the town were excited as to how they were portrayed. Ricky, in turn, was applauded by the council throughout the town for the marvelous job that he had done.

That night, he received a call from the young man who had violated the first design. Ricky forgave him and invited him to come and work on his next project.

Ricky was initially disgusted and upset by what he thought was a disaster, but through the grace of God and the presence of the Holy Spirit, Ricky did not despair long. He got up, went back to the site, and was able to see what he did not see initially once he turned the mural around.

So often, when we are in despair, we, like Ricky, can't see beyond our grief, but God, the designer of all creations, always has an alternative plan. Let us not ever tune Him out. Thank You, Lord, for the alternative that proved to be better than the original. *Amen.*

Lord, Please Give Me Strength

....

I can do all things through Him
who gives me strength.
—Philippians 4:13

....

Carolyn was in her office working on the end-of-the-year report when her phone rang. She said to her secretary, "Please get it, I am so tired, and I feel like I'm being stretched too thin and pulled so tight that I can't do anymore."

Carolyn was a leader in her church. She was president of the women's ministry group, a Sunday school teacher for the primary children, served once a month as an usher, and was asked to join the altar guild but had not as of yet confirmed.

She was tired, and her job as supervisor of the first-year teachers for the school district was more than enough, but she went through with her commitments and did her job well. So well that the phone call was from the superintendent of schools asking for a conference with her. She set the appointment up for Friday, and not knowing what he wanted, she was a bit puzzled but not too concerned.

When she arrived home, she put her things away and vowed to not do any work, and that's when the phone rang; it was Pastor Jones asking if it was a good time to talk, and she said yes.

Pastor Jones was in a dilemma; the speaker for youth Sunday had overbooked and could not speak, and he asked if she would step in.

Carolyn had not prayed at all that day; she jumped up out of bed with thoughts on her mind and had not spoken to God. She said to the pastor, "Let me pray about it."

When she got off of the phone, she prayed and asked God to lead her and fell right off to sleep, mentally fatigued.

She kept running over in her mind what the pastor had asked and was waiting for God to respond. In the meantime, she went to her meeting with the superintendent, and he said that the new teachers that she was supervising needed a day retreat and that he felt that she could organize it.

She left the meeting so overwhelmed, feeling pulled even tighter than before. The superintendent was her boss; this was her job, she could not say no, yet her pastor was waiting for a response.

When she arrived home, she slumped down on the sofa, and as she opened her mail, there was a note from her sister, Elvira, with a card that was printed with the scripture on the outside, the words from Philippians 4:13, "I can do all things through Christ that strengthens me." Carolyn quickly called her and thanked her for the card. She explained to Elvira how she was feeling and the dilemma she thought she was in and how she prayed for an answer. The card was just what she needed. She called the pastor and said yes, and the next day, she began the work on the retreat and replied to the superintendent that she would organize the retreat but would not lead it. He agreed, and she felt relieved.

Many times, we may feel overwhelmed and pulled in many directions, but by the grace of God, we can do all things through He, who gives us all the strength that is needed. Thank You, Lord! *Amen.*

EVERYDAY
CHALLENGES

Tired of Being Tired

Come to me, all who are weary and are burdened
and I will give you rest. Take my yoke upon you,
and learn from me, for I am gentle and humble
in heart, and you will find rest for your souls.
For my yoke is easy, and my burden is light.
—Matthew 11:28-30

Charlotte came into the house and threw her mask on the counter, and said, "I'm tired of this mask. I'm tired of washing my hands, and I'm tired of social distancing. This pandemic has cost me my job, my car is soon to be repossessed, the mortgage is three months late, food is limited, the kids are stir-crazy, and I'm just darn tired." She said, "I have prayed and prayed and prayed, but no change. Pastor Roy has given us donations from members, and we are grateful, but it's not enough. The line at the food pantry today was horrible. There was bickering going on between two women because one was too close to the another. It's apparent that the longer the pandemic lasts, the grumpier people are getting."

All Charlotte could do was to put the few things she received away. Tired and exhausted from standing in the food line, she sat down in front of her Bible and read what she had been reading for months. Matthew 25:35–36, "For I was hungry and you gave me something to eat, I was thirsty and you gave me something to drink, I was a stranger and you invited me in, I needed clothes and you clothed me, I was sick and you looked after me, I was in prison and you came to visit me." As she read those words again, she broke down and cried out to God, "My children and I are hungry, thirsty, naked, and sick, I need help." She closed her Bible and just rocked back and forth, staring off into space.

Her youngest child, observing his mom, came over and hugged her. He said, "Mommy, don't cry, didn't you tell me when I said that I was hungry that God will provide. Remember when the doorbell rang and our neighbor, Ms. Gladys, brought us two pizzas and soda, and after we ate, I was no longer hungry?"

"Mommy," he said, "just watch, God will provide what we need, so we can't stop praying because God loves us so much, and we just have to wait."

Charlotte dried her eyes, prepared dinner with what she had, and listened to her son praying and waiting.

Over time, the pandemic cases slowed down. Things improved as well when the stimulus check arrived. By the grace of God, Charlotte found a new job, and life now is a lot better. As we all go through this pandemic, let us not lose faith in God. He has not deserted us and is available to all. We must, during this time, as well seek him out, keep praying, and read our Bibles. He waits, He listens, and He provides. *Amen.*

No Sleight of Hand with Jesus

Has not My hand made all these things?
—Acts 7:50

Magicians are thought to always have a trick up their sleeves. They make things disappear and then reappear. There are times that they are so tricky that we can't believe our eyes and wonder how he or she did what they did. And what was done was called magic or sleight of hand, and the hand was quicker than the eye.

During the time that Jesus was on earth, it was thought many times that he was a magician. He calmed the sea, multiplied five loaves of bread and two fish, and fed five thousand men plus women and children. He walked on water, rebuked Satan, healed the sick, raised the dead, opened the eyes of the blind, along with many other miracles, and with all that He did, He was despised and rejected by many.

He was thought to be a witch or have powers given to Him by Satan. He was not believable, even though people saw what He did with their own eyes.

As we read the stories of Jesus and see the healings of people in our day, do we believe in the power of God to do what we want Him to do?

When people are healed of cancer, is that magic? When the doctor performs surgery and repairs a limb, is that magic? When we are healed with a virus, is that magic? No!

Jesus, through the grace of God, like the Holy Spirit, has been given the authority of God to do what we see and more. Jesus is no magician; He is the Son of God sent to show us the way. Let us understand that when healings and things happen to us or others, let us not say we are lucky, but let us say that through the grace and power of God, we are healed and restored. There was no magician with magic hands; it was with hands gifted by God that brought change to the situation presented.

When we accept God and accept His Son, we can say, "Yes, Lord, I believe and know that through the power of the Holy Spirit that all things will work together for good for those who love the Lord" (Romans 8:28).

Let us now believe in He who came to bring salvation for all. There was no trick, sleight of hand, nor magic to His coming nor leaving, and there is no trick to His promised return. Do I believe it? "Yes," and I pray that you do too! *Amen.*

Please, Lord, Wake Me Up

I lie down and sleep; I wake again,
because the Lord sustains me.
> —Psalm 3:5

Edith came home from work and plopped herself on the sofa. She had stopped at the local deli and bought a sandwich and soda, and that was supper. Edith had no get-up and go. It appeared to have gotten up and gone. Her friends could not encourage her to go out. Her mom called her several times throughout the week to invite her over for supper, but she declined, saying, "I have no initiative to do anything." She was called lazy, selfish, and non-caring.

With all that was said, Edith was not moved until her sister came over to the apartment to talk to her. She pointed out that Edith's house was a mess. She noted Edith's lack of care for herself and that she was disheveled. She also said that Edith was not fulfilling her commitments at church. She had joined the altar guild, choir, and Sunday school but was no longer participating because she was too busy.

That night, Edith had a dream. In the dream, she was walking with a woman who she did not know but knew her well. She told her about her life, the schools she attended, the boyfriends she had in her past, her present job, and her lack of initiative. She pointed out that she had turned away from her family, friends, church, and God because her last relationship was a downer and left her depressed.

The woman said that her life was blessed by God and that the true love of her life was not her boyfriend but Jesus, who said that He would be with her. He didn't criticize her, talk negatively, call her names, exploit her, nor leave her high and dry owing her money. She explained that the love of Jesus was free and that He paid the debt for all our sins and loved us regardless of our faults. And just as the woman appeared, she left.

Edith woke up shaken and wondered about the woman and the dream. She tried to go back to sleep but was restless and was not able to sleep, so she got up, and tidied up the apartment. She took a long hot shower and washed her hair. She looked in her closet and found an outfit that she had not worn in a long time. She went so far as to put on a little makeup.

This went on the entire week. What was so surprising was that on Sunday, she went to church and sat next to her family, who was so happy and surprised to see her.

The pastor's message came from John 14:26, "But the Advocate, the Holy Spirit, whom the Father will send in my name, will teach you all things and will remind you of everything I have said to you."

As he spoke, Edith remembered her dream and knew then that the woman in the dream was sent by God to inspire and encourage her. She knew that Jesus loved her, that she was not a failure, and that her worth was not based on the opinion of another. After service, she went to the director of the altar guild and promised to resume her call to service.

She went to her mom's house for dinner and felt so happy. When she went home that night, instead of flopping on the sofa, she looked at her Bible, which was opened to the baptism of Jesus. She read the words from Mark 1:11, "You are my Son, whom I love; with you I am well pleased." With tears streaming down her face, she prayed, "Lord, I am Your daughter. I pray for You to be well pleased with me. Thank You for the message sent by the Holy Spirit in my dream, and thank You for Your love." *Amen.*

Can You Hear Me?

Then I heard the voice of the Lord, saying,
"Whom shall I send, and who will go for
Us?" and I said, "Here am I. Send me!"
—Isaiah 6:8

Eunice was having difficulty hearing and noticed it more so when she attended a conference for cafeteria workers. She then made an appointment to see an audiologist. After the evaluation, the audiologist told her that there was a hearing loss and recommended that she consider wearing hearing aids. Eunice went home and discussed it with her husband, who was in great favor of the aids because many times he had spoken to her, and she had not responded.

When Eunice was not heard, she was in the dark as to what was being said. We, too, are many times in the dark and miss out on things happening around us because of not hearing; we are not focused and will tune people out, miss assignments, and not follow up or follow through on requests.

We do the same thing to God and don't hear the voice spoken through the Holy Spirit. God speaks to us, and the devil speaks as well. The difference is that God will not lead us to do anything that would hurt, harm, or endanger ourselves or others. On the other hand, the devil will say things loudly and offer things that we know are not right, yet so tempting that it hurts our relationship with God and affects our walk.

Our hearing and tuning in to the Holy Spirit do not require ears. It requires our souls to be open to hearing God as He speaks. His voice is distinctive. It's one that is always recognizable, and just as a baby recognizes the voice of his mother, we, over time, as our love and relationship grow, will recognize more and more the voice of our God. Thank You, God, for souls open to You. *Amen.*

God Walks with Us in the Valley of Darkness

*Even though I walk through the darkest
valley, I will fear no evil, for you are with me;
your rod and your staff, they comfort me.*
— Psalm 23:4

It was early morning, and Anita was driving to the park for her morning walk. As she turned to get onto the main road, she was blinded by the early morning sun. She noticed that the traffic had slowed down and that cars were moving at a snail's pace. The glare of the sun was so bright, and there was no visibility except for the white line on the road. She continued slowly and turned off at the first exit, and the sun was now at her back. She thought as she made her way to the park, that we become blinded when we take our eyes off God.

The blessing is that even though we go through the valleys of darkness and are blinded by what it offers that our Father God never deserts us. He is with us, and when we become lost, disoriented, and see how dark life really is and what we have sunk into, our loving Father clears the glare, grabs our hands, and lovingly guides us safely to our destination. Thank You, dear God, for guiding us through the glares that distract us from You. *Amen.*

Praying Specific Prayers

And pray in the Spirit on all occasions
with all kinds of prayers and requests. With
this in mind, be alert and always keep
on praying for all the Lord's people.
　　　　　　　　　　　　—Ephesians 6:18

"I feel neglected," Alyssa said to her friend Marie. "I have prayed and prayed and prayed for over a month for a new car, and God has not responded."

Marie said, "Alyssa, were you specific as to the car you wanted?"

"Yes," she said.

"Did you tell God the color, style, and year?"

"Yes, I did," Alyssa said in disgust. "I even told Him that I needed it last week, and He did not come through."

Marie said, "Alyssa, God is not in the car dealership business. He hears our prayers and answers them according to His plan and even our finances. God knows the kind of payments that are within your means. He knows that your job is temporary and that you are having difficulty paying rent and not even sticking to a budget. Why would God just hand you a car that you can't afford? My sister," Marie said, "God loves us deeply, but there are times when He has to show His love by not fulfilling our prayer request. Many times when He gives us what we pray for in a few months, we return to him crying out, saying, 'God, please help me, I can't pay my bills.' Let us understand that, out of love, God protects us and our credit as well so that when the time is right, we will receive what we pray for. So keep driving what you can take care of it, and in time, your prayer will be answered."

Alyssa's story is a story of many. We pray for that which we don't need nor can afford. God neither rejects nor abandons us. He will not give us that which will hurt us. Let us pray to God to open our eyes to His glory and look at what we have and not rush into that which is not needed today.

Our tomorrows are coming, and God is in them like He is in our todays. Today, apparently, is not the day for many prayers to be answered. Keep praying; God is still listening. Don't give up.

Thank You, Lord, for answering prayers at the appointed time. *Amen.*

About the Authors

Rev. H. Jocelyn Irving is a senior partner and chief spiritual officer of Our Faithful Walk with God Ministry, LLC. She is the former associate rector of St. Luke's Episcopal Church in Montclair, New Jersey, and is a retired rector of the Episcopal Church of the Atonement in Washington, DC. She was, for twenty-four years, an educator in the Paterson, New Jersey, public-school system while attending Drew University, obtaining her master of divinity degree. She is the proud mother of Vian, Farrah (Douglas), Herman III, and Christopher and grandmother of NahDirah, Vian, Nia, Jordan, Christian, Saniah, Christopher II, and Scarlet.

Obie Pinckney is a senior partner and chief strategy officer of Our Faithful Walk with God Ministry, LLC. He is a retired business owner, lawyer, and government executive and an outspoken disciple of Jesus Christ. He earned degrees from South Carolina State University, American University, and Georgetown University Law Center. A resident of Glenarden, Maryland, he is the husband of Carolyn—father of Pennye and Pamela (Alphonso); grandfather of Nichelle, Nia, and Natalie; and great-grandfather of Zora.

CPSIA information can be obtained
at www.ICGtesting.com
Printed in the USA
BVHW040934070423
661946BV00006B/159

9 781684 988518